The Greatest Hits From The Disco Era

Project Manager: Zobeida Pérez
Project Consultant: Larry Kornblum
Book Art Design: Carmen Fortunato

© 2000 WARNER BROS. PUBLICATIONS
All Rights Reserved

Any duplication, adaptation or arrangement of the compositions
contained in this collection requires the written consent of the Publisher.
No part of this book may be photocopied or reproduced in any way without permission.
Unauthorized uses are an infringement of the U.S. Copyright Act and are punishable by law.

CONTENTS

BOOGIE FEVER	The Sylvers	8
BOOGIE NIGHTS	Heatwave	12
BOOGIE SHOES	KC and the Sunshine Band	16
BOOGIE WONDERLAND	Earth, Wind & Fire with The Emotions	19
CAR WASH	Rose Royce	30
CELEBRATION	Kool & the Gang	35
DANCING QUEEN	Abba	38
DISCO DUCK (Part I)	Rick Dees & His Cast of Idiots	42
DISCO LADY	Do Re Mi	50
DON'T LEAVE ME THIS WAY	Thelma Houston	56
ELECTRIC SLIDE A/K/A ELECTRIC BOOGIE	Marcia Griffiths	62
GET DOWN TONIGHT	KC and the Sunshine Band	66
GOODTIMES A/K/A/ RAPPER'S DELIGHT	Chic	69
HEAVEN MUST BE MISSING AN ANGEL	Tavares	72
(Your Love Has Lifted Me) HIGHER AND HIGHER	Rita Coolidge	77
HOT LINE	The Sylvers	80
THE HUSTLE	Van McCoy	85
I LOVE MUSIC	The O'Jays	180
I WILL SURVIVE	Gloria Gaynor	3
I'M YOUR BOOGIE MAN	KC and the Sunshine Band	92
IT ONLY TAKES A MINUTE	Tavares	96
IT'S RAINING MEN	The Weather Girls	106
JUNGLE BOOGIE	Kool & the Gang	104
KEEP IT COMIN' LOVE	KC and the Sunshine Band	114
KNOCK ON WOOD	Amii Stewart	99
LADIES NIGHT	Kool & the Gang	118
LADY LOVE	Lou Rawls	132
LE FREAK	Chic	144
MacARTHUR PARK	Donna Summer	122
MORE, MORE, MORE (Part 1)	Andrea True Connection	88
RING MY BELL	Anita Ward	147
ROCK THE BOAT	The Hues Corporation	150
ROCK YOUR BABY	George McCrae	27
(Shake, Shake, Shake) SHAKE YOUR BOOTY	KC and the Sunshine Band	155
SHAKE YOUR GROOVE THING	Peaches & Herb	160
THAT'S THE WAY (I Like It)	KC and the Sunshine Band	24
TSOP (The Sound of Philadelphia)	MFSB featuring The Three Degrees	176
TURN THE BEAT AROUND	Vicki Sue Robinson	167
WE ARE FAMILY	Sister Sledge	172
WHEN WILL I SEE YOU AGAIN	The Three Degrees	139
YOU MAKE ME FEEL LIKE DANCING	Leo Sayer	46

BOOGIE NIGHTS

Words and Music by
ROD TEMPERTON

Boogie Nights - 4 - 1

© 1981 RODSONGS
All Rights Administered by ALMO MUSIC CORP. (ASCAP)
All Rights Reserved

BOOGIE WONDERLAND

Words and Music by
JOHN LIND and ALLEE WILLIS

Boogie Wonderland - 5 - 1

© 1979 EMI BLACKWOOD MUSIC INC., BIG MYSTIQUE MUSIC
and IRVING MUSIC, INC. (BMI)
All Rights Reserved

THAT'S THE WAY (I LIKE IT)

Words and Music by
HARRY CASEY and RICHARD FINCH

ROCK YOUR BABY

Words and Music by
HARRY CASEY and RICHARD FINCH

CAR WASH

Words and Music by
NORMAN WHITFIELD

Car Wash - 5 - 1

© 1976 Universal - Duchess Music Corporation
All Rights Reserved

32

Car Wash - 5 - 3

CELEBRATION

**Words and Music by
RONALD BELL, CLAYDES SMITH, GEORGE BROWN,
JAMES TAYLOR, ROBERT MICKENS, EARL TOON,
DENNIS THOMAS, ROBERT BELL and EUMIR DEODATO**

Moderately ♩ = 116

(1.-4.; 6.8. Instr. only)
5.7. Cel - e - brate good times, come on!

There's a par-ty go-ing on right here; a cel-e-bra-tion to last through-out the years; so bring your good times,___ and your

Celebration - 3 - 1

© 1980, 1994 WARNER-TAMERLANE PUBLISHING CORP., SECOND DECADE MUSIC CO. and WB MUSIC CORP.
All Rights on behalf of SECOND DECADE MUSIC CO. Administered by WARNER-TAMERLANE PUBLISHING CORP.
All Rights Reserved

Dancing Queen

Words and Music by
BENNY ANDERSON, STIG ANDERSON
and BJÖRN ULVAEUS

DISCO DUCK (PART 1)

Words and Music by
RICK DEES

Mov-in' my feet to the Dis-co beat,
Flap-pin' my arms, I be-gin to cluck.

1. how in the world could I keep my seat?

2. Look at me! I'm the Dis-co Duck! *(recite like Donald Duck)* Oh, get down, mama. I got to have me a woman.

Disco Duck (Part 1) - 4 - 2

Dis - co, Dis - co Duck. Dis - co, Dis - co Duck. Try your luck; don't be a cluck. Dis - co, Dis - co, Dis - co, Dis - co. Dis - co, Dis - co Duck. Dis - co, Dis - co Duck. *(recite like Donald Duck)* Oh, get down, mama.

Oh, mama, shake your tail feathers.

When the music stopped I returned to my seat, but there's no stoppin' a duck and his beat. So I got back up to try my luck.

D.S. 𝄋 (vocal ad lib) and fade

Why, look! *(recite like Donald Duck)* Everybody's doin' the

YOU MAKE ME FEEL LIKE DANCING

Words and Music by
LEO SAYER and VINCENT PONCIA

Moderate Disco beat

You've got a cute way of talk - ing;
Quar - ter to four in the morn - ing,

you got the bet - ter of me. ___ Just snap your fin - gers and I'm
I ain't feel - ing tired, no, no, no. ___ Just hold me tight and leave on

walk - ing like a dog hang-ing on your lead.
the light, 'cause I don't wan-na go home.

I'm in a spin, you know; shak-ing on a string, you know.
You put a spell on me; I'm right where you want me to be.

You make me feel like danc - ing; I wan-na dance the night a-way.

You make me feel like danc - ing; I'm gon-na dance the night a-way.

You make me feel like dancing. I feel like dancing, dancing, dance the night away. I feel like dancing, dancing, ah.

dancing, dancing, dance the night away. I feel like

dancing, dancing, dance the night away. I feel like dancing, dancing, ah.

And if you'll let me stay, we'll dance our lives a-way.

Repeat and fade

You make me feel like danc-ing; I wan-na dance my life a-way.

You make me feel like danc-ing; I wan-na dance my life a-way.

DISCO LADY

Words and Music by
HARVEY SCALES, AL VANCE
and DON DAVIS

Moderate Disco beat

Shake it up, shake it down; move it in, move it 'round, dis-co la-dy. Move it in, move it out; move it

© 1976 EMI LONGITUDE MUSIC and EMI FULL KEEL MUSIC
All Rights Reserved

in and about, dis-co la-dy. ___ Shake it up, shake it down; move it in, move it out, dis-co la-dy. ___ Hey, sex-y la-dy, ___ said I like the way you move your thang. ___ Lord, have mer-cy, girl. ___ You dance so fine, and you're right on

time. Girl, you ought to be on T. V. on Soul Train. When you get the groove, it ain't no stop-pin'. Just can't help it; I'm fin-ger pop-pin'. Shake it up, shake it down; move it in, move it 'round, dis-co la-dy. Move it in, move it 'round; move it in, 'round a-bout, dis-co la-dy.

Shake it, ba-by, shake it. Ba-by, shake your thang. Shake it, ba-by, shake it.

F#7

Ba-by, shake your thang. You got me groov-in', I feel like mov-in'.

B9   **A7**

You got me mov-in',

can't sit still I'm groov-in'. _____ I like that funk-y stuff! Shake it

Coda
Hey, sex-y la-dy! _____

Girl, you drive me cra-zy. _____ You dance so

fine, and you're right on time. Girl, you drive me right your of my mind.

If it wasn't for the girl sittin' next to me, I'd jump right up and out-ta my safe-ty seat, You got me hyp-no-tized; soul mes-mor-ized. Girl, you're mov-in' me. Girl, you're groov-in' me.

Repeat and fade
G6

DON'T LEAVE ME THIS WAY

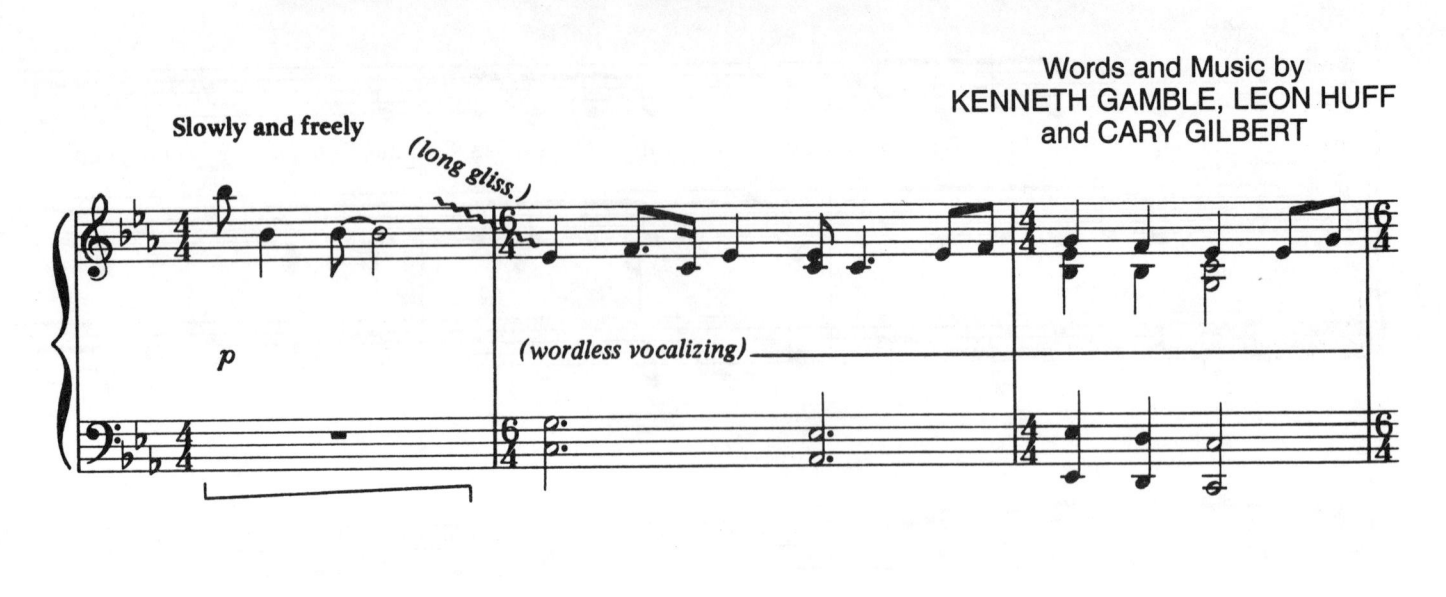

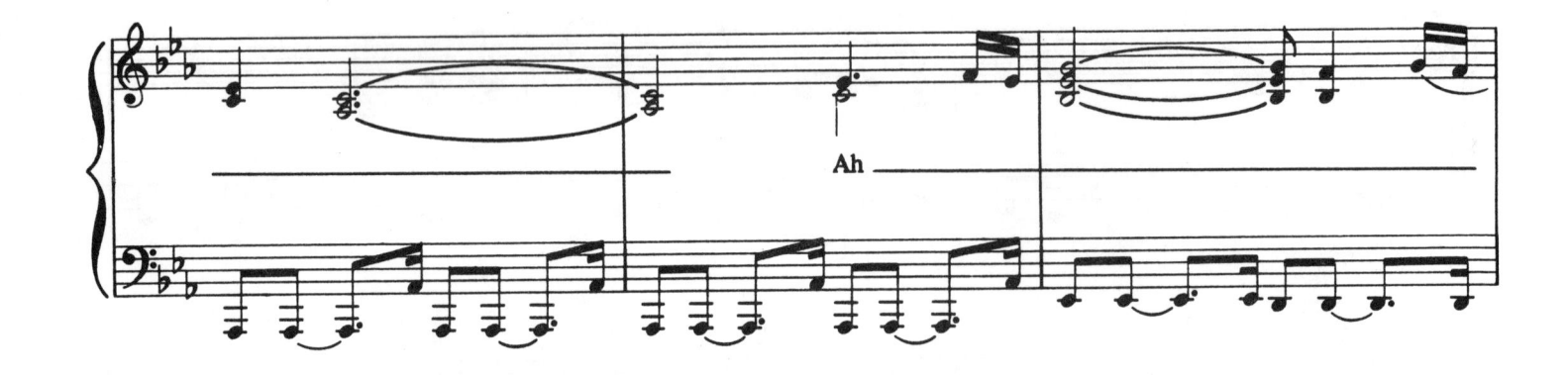

Words and Music by
KENNETH GAMBLE, LEON HUFF
and CARY GILBERT

*Bass figure may be simplified by playing ¼ notes throughout

Guitar → (Capo up 3 frets)
Piano →
Am D G G7
Cm F Bb Bb7
Don't leave me this way; I can't sur-
mp
C G Am Dm7
Eb Bb Cm Fm7
vive, I can't stay a - live with - out your love.
Dm7/G Am D G
Fm7/Bb Cm F Bb
Oh ba - by, don't leave me this way;
G7 C G Am
Bb7 Eb Bb Cm
I can't ex - ist, I'll sure - ly miss

Dm7
Fm7
Dm7/G
Fm7/Bb
A
C
your ten - der kiss.
Don't leave me this way.
A
C
G
Bb
D
F
A
C
Ba - by, my heart is full of love and de - sire for you! Now
f
G
Bb
D
F
A
C
come on down and do what cha got - ta do! You
G
Bb
D
F
A
C
start - ed this fire down in my soul! Now

can't you see__ it's burn - in'__ out - ta con - trol?

Come on sat - is - fy__ the need in me, 'cause

on - ly your good lov - in' can set me free!__

Don't, don't you leave_ me this way,__ no.

G7
Bb7
C
Eb
Don't you un - der - stand? I'm
G
Bb
Am
Cm
Dm7
Fm7
at your com - mand. Oh ba - by, please,
G7
Bb7
Am
Cm
Dm7
Fm7
G
Bb
3
please don't leave me this way. No ba - by,
Am
Cm
D
F
G
Bb
G7
Bb7
don't leave me this way, no; I can't sur -

vive, ___ I can't stay a-live ___ with-out your love. ___

Ba-by, don't leave me this way

D.S. al Coda

Oh now

Coda

set me free!

Repeat and fade

(with vocal ad libs)

ELECTRIC SLIDE
a/k/a ELECTRIC BOOGIE

Words and Music by
NEVILLE LIVINGSTON

Moderately ♩ = 92

Chorus:

1.3. You can't see it. (It's e-lec-tric.)
2. *See additional lyrics*

You've got to feel it. (It's e-lec-tric.) Oo, it's shock-ing. (It's e-

Electric Slide - 4 - 1

© 1984 SOLOMONIC MUSIC
Administered by TAFARI MUSIC INC. (ASCAP)
All Rights Reserved

lec-tric.) Rap: Dig Miss Kelly with electric belly. She's moving with electric, she sure got the boogie.

You got-ta know__ it, (It's e-lec-tric, boog-ie woog-ie, woog-ie.) that you can't__ hold__ it. (It's e-lec-tric, boog-ie woog-ie, woog-ie.) But you know it's there,__ here, there, and ev-'ry-where.__

64

Verse:

1. I've got to move.___ I'm going on a
2.3.4. *See additional lyrics*

par-ty ride. I've got to groove,___ groove,___ groove,___

and from this mu-sic I___ just can't hide.

1.3. | *2.* *D.S. %* | *4.* *D.C. al Coda*

2. Are you com-ing 2. Some
4. I've got to

Electric Slide - 4 - 3

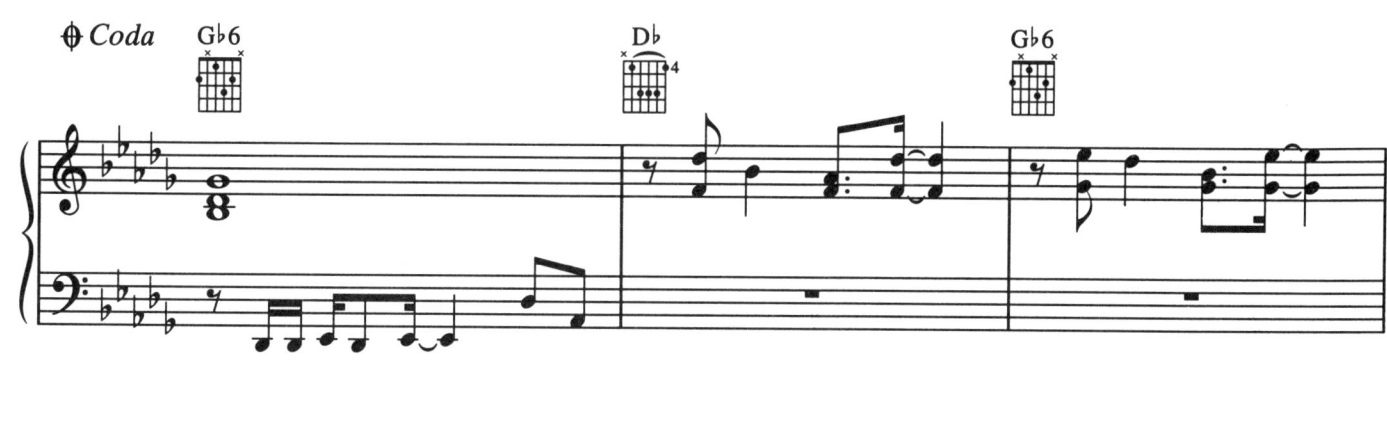

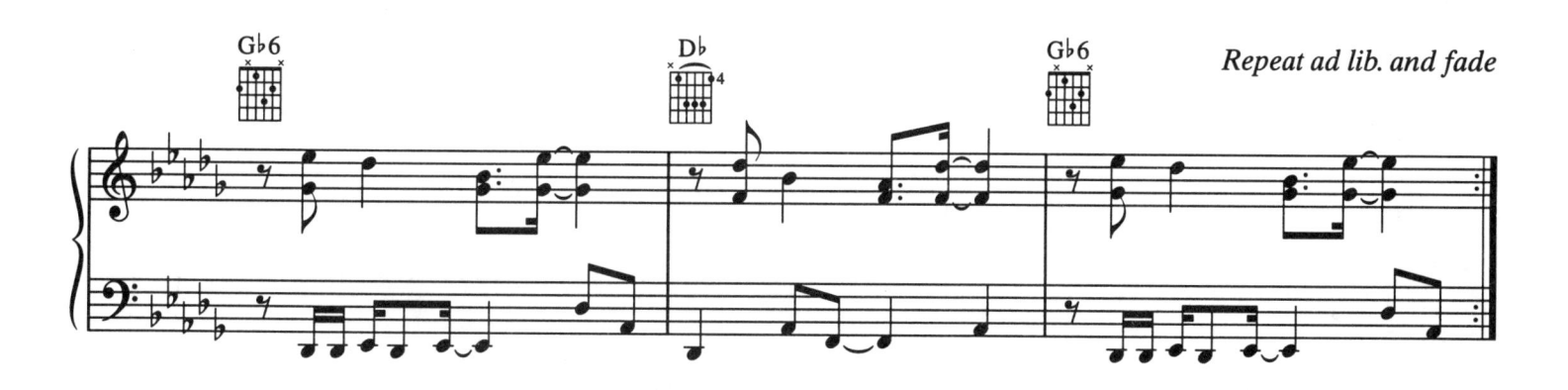

Verse 2:
Are you coming with me?
Come, let me take you on a party ride,
And I'll teach you, teach you, teach you,
I'll teach you the electric slide.

Chorus 2:
Some say it's a mystic.
It's electric, boogie woogie, woogie.
You can't resist it.
It's electric, boogie woogie, woogie.
You can't do without it.
It's electric, boogie woogie, woogie.
Rap:
Say to dig Miss Molly.
She's feeling jolly.
She's moving with electric.
She sure got to boogie.
Don't want to lose it.
It's electric, boogie woogie, woogie.
You got to use it.
It's electric, boogie woogie, woogie.
But you know it's there,
Here, there, and ev'rywhere.

Verse 3:
Instrumental

Verse 4:
I've got to move.
Come, let me take you on a party ride,
And I'll teach you, teach you, teach you,
I'll teach you the electric slide.

GET DOWN TONIGHT

Words and Music by
HARRY CASEY and
RICHARD FINCH

Moderate, with a strong beat

Ba - by, babe _____ let's get to - geth - er _____ hon - ey, hon - ey _____ me and
Ba - by, babe _____ I'll meet you _____ same place, _____ same time

you _____ and do the things _____ oh _____ do the things _____ and
where we can _____ oh _____ get to - geth - er and

that we like to do. _____ Oh do a lit - tle dance, make a lit - tle love, get
ease up our mind. _____

© 1975 EMI LONGITUDE MUSIC
All Rights Reserved

F11
F
F11
down to-night,
get down to-night.
Do a lit-tle dance,
B♭
F11
1. F
2. F
make a lit-tle love,
get down to-night,
get down to-night.
down to-night ba-by
F11
B♭
F11
Do a lit-tle dance,
make a lit-tle love,
get down to-night,
get
1. F
2. F
F11
F
down to-night.
down to-night ba-by

F11
F
F
Get down, get down, get down,
F
get down, get down to - night ba - by wo wo wo
wo wo wo wo wo wo wo
F
Get down, get down, get down,
get down, get down to - night ba - by na na na
1.
na na na na na na na
2. F
ba - by this ve - ry min - ute child oh
D.S. and fade

Good Times
a/k/a RAPPER'S DELIGHT

Words and Music by
BERNARD EDWARDS and NILE ROGERS

these are the good times. ___ Our new state of mind. ___

These are the good times. ___

Hap-py days are here a-gain. The time is right for
A ru-mor has it that it's get-ting late. Time march-es on;

mak-in' friends. Let's get to-geth-er. How 'bout a quar-ter to ten?
just can't wait. The clock keeps turn-in'. Why hes-i-tate?

[A7sus4] Come to-mor-row, let's all do it a-gain. [A13] [Em7] Boys will be boys. Bet-ter
You sil-ly fool, you can't change your fate. Let's cut the rug; lit-tle

let them have their toys. [A7sus4] Girls will be girls. [A13] Cute po-ny-tails and curls.
jive and jit-ter-bug. We want the best. We won't set-tle for less.

[Em7] Must put an end to this stress and strife. [A7sus4] I think I want to live the
Don't be a drag. Par-tic-i-pate. Clams on the half-shell and

1. [A13] sport-ing life. Good times, roll-er skates, 2. [A13] roll-er skates. Good times,

D.S. and fade

Good Times a/k/a Rapper's Delight - 3 - 3

HEAVEN MUST BE MISSING AN ANGEL

Words and Music by
FREDERICK PERREN and KENNETH ST. LEWIS

Moderately

Heav-en must be miss-ing an an-gel, miss-ing an an-gel, child, 'cause you're here with me right now. Your love is heav-en-ly, ba-by,

Heaven Must Be Missing an Angel - 5 - 1

© 1976 Universal - PolyGram International Publishing, Inc., Perren-Vibes Music Inc.,
Universal - Songs of PolyGram International, Inc. and Bull Pen Music, Inc.
All Rights Reserved

Dm7 Dm7/G C Dm7 Dm7/G C
heav-en-ly to me, ba - by, Your kiss,
Dm7 Dm7/G C Dm7 Dm7/G
filled with ten - der - ness; I want all I can
C Dm7 Dm7/G C
get of your sex - i - ness.
Dm7 Dm7/G C Dm7 Dm7/G
Show - ers, your love comes in

showers, and ev-'ry ho-ur on the ho-ur.

you let me feel your lov-in' pow-er.

There's a rain-bow o-ver my shoul-der; when you came, my cup run-neth o-ver, You gave me your heav-en-ly love, and if one night you hear cryin' from above, it's 'cause heaven must be missing an angel, missing an angel, child, 'cause you're here with me right now.

Your love is heavenly, baby, heavenly to

C
Dm7
Dm7/G
C
me, ba - by,
Heav - en
Dm7
Dm7/G
Dm7
G
Play 4 times
I'm cap - tured by your spell,
Dm7
G
Em7
you're dif-f'rent, girl, I can tell.
When you're lay-in' on my
Am
Dm7
G
F
Em7
Dm7
D.S. and Fade
pil-low ba - by,
a - bove your pret-ty head there's a ha - lo. That's why I know

(Your Love Has Lifted Me)
HIGHER AND HIGHER

Words and Music by
GARY JACKSON, CARL SMITH
and RAYNARD MINER

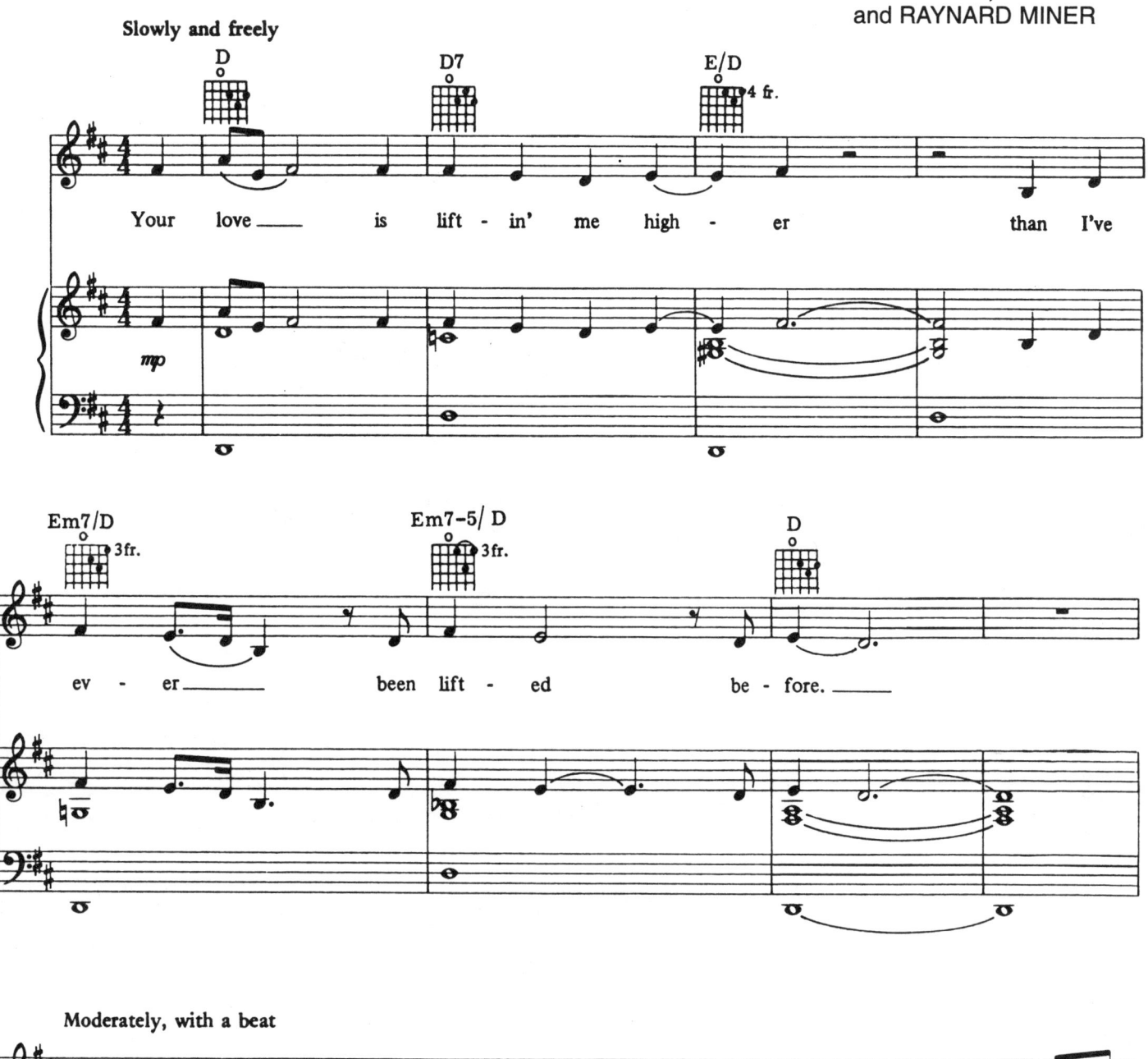

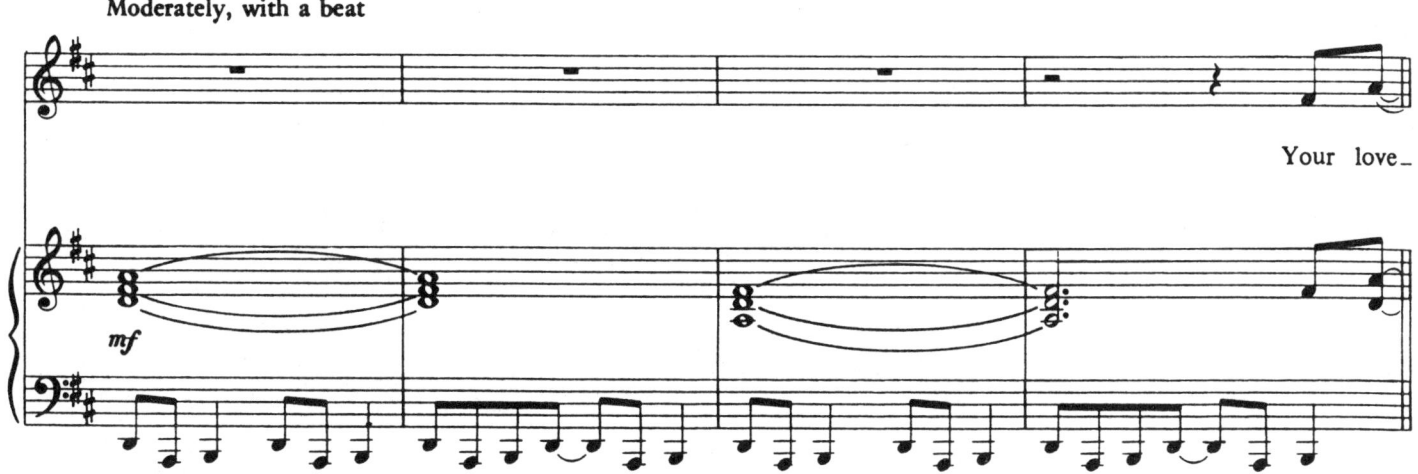

Slowly and freely

Your love ___ is liftin' me high - er than I've ev - er ___ been lift - ed be - fore. ___

Moderately, with a beat

Your love ___

Higher and Higher - 3 - 1

© 1967 CHEVIS MUSIC, INC., WARNER-TAMERLANE PUBLISHING CORP. and UNICHAPPELL MUSIC INC.
All Rights Reserved

D
Em7/D
3fr.
is lift - in' me high - er than I've ev -
I was down - heart - ed; dis - ap - point-
Em7-5/D
D
er been lift - ed be - fore. So keep it
ment was my clos - est friend. But you
Em7/D
up, quench my de - sire, and I'll be
came; he soon de - part - ed, and he
Em7-5/D
D
1.
at your side for - ev - er - more. Now once
nev - er showed his face a - gain.

2.
D
E/D
4 fr.
I'm _ so glad _ I fi - nal - ly found _ you;
Em7/D
3fr.
Em7-5/D
3fr.
D
you're that "one _ in a mil - lion" man. _
E/D
4 fr.
When you wrap _ your lov - in' arms a - round _ me,
Em7/D
3fr
Em7-5/D
3fr.
D
D.S.𝄋 (lyric 1) and fade
I can stand _ up and face _ the world _ a - gain. _ Your love _

HOT LINE

Words and Music by
FREDERICK PERREN and
KENNETH ST. LEWIS

Moderately

Hot line, hot line, calling on the hot line ___ for your love ___ for your love. ___ Hot line, hot line, calling on the hot line, ___ on the hot ___ line. ___

Hot Line - 5 - 1

© 1976 Universal - PolyGram International Publishing, Inc., Perren-Vibes Music Inc.,
Universal - Songs of PolyGram International, Inc. and Bull Pen Music, Inc.
All Rights Reserved

I'm call-ing on the hot line for your love. Ba-by 'cause I'm burn-in' up like a house on fire, my de-sire is climb-in' high-er, ba-by, woo. Girl, the way you move your lips I can tell
Op-er-a-tor, ex-cuse me. Please, this is more

you got fire in your kiss.
than an e-mer-gen-cy.

The way you flash your eyes looks like light-
Take those phones off of your ears, this is on-

-nin' light-ing up the sky.
-ly for my ba-by to hear.

Stop all the calls in the world till I get you, girl, catch you at home.

I asked the C. I. A. if it was okay to use their private phone. Woo, Oh, baby, baby, Hot line, hot line, calling on the hot line for your love, for your love. Hot line, hot line, calling on the hot line __ on the hot __ line. __ __ line, __ ba-by.

Where are you? __ Here am I. __
Don't keep it bus-y, don't make me diz-zy. __

Should I get in touch with the F. B. I.? I know my call __
Your love makes me want to shout, "You're my lov-er, __

1st time - D.S.
2nd time - D.S. and Fade

will be ac-cept-ed; there's no chance __ of be-ing dis-con-nect-ed on the
un-der cov-er," __ you know what __ I'm talk-ing a-bout.

THE HUSTLE

By VAN McCOY

F
Gm7
3fr
F
Gm7
3fr
B♭maj7
F/A
Gm7
3fr
B♭/C
F
Gm7
3fr
F
Gm7
3fr
B♭maj7
F/A
Gm7
3fr
B♭/C
D♭maj7
4fr
B♭m9

Do the Hus-tle!

The Hustle - 3 - 3

MORE, MORE, MORE (PART 1)

Words and Music by
GREGG DIAMOND

Ooo, _____ How do you like ___ your love? Ooo, _____

More, More, More (Part 1) - 4 - 1

© 1976 EMI U CATALOG INC.,
BMG SONGS INC. and MUSIC RESOURCES INTERNATIONAL CORP.
Print Rights for EMI U CATALOG INC. Administered by
WARNER BROS. PUBLICATIONS U.S. INC.
All Rights Reserved

Fmaj7
— How do you like — your love?
Bb
But if you want — to know — how I real - ly feel, —
G7
get the cam - 'ras roll - in'; get the ac - tion go - in'.
Bb
Ba - by, you know — my love for you — is real, — so

take me where you want to. Man, my heart you steal.___ More, more,___ more.___

How do you like___ it? How do you like___ it? More, more,___ more.___

How do you like___ it? How do you like___ it? More, more,___ more.___

How do you like___ it? How do you like___ it?

How do you like_it? How do you like_your love?

D.S. %% and Fade at Chorus

More, More, More (Part 1) - 4 - 4

I'M YOUR BOOGIE MAN

Words and Music by
HARRY CASEY and RICHARD FINCH

Steady Disco Beat

I'm your boo-gie man,___ that's what I am.___ I'm here to do___ what-ev-er I can. Be it ear-ly morn-ing, late

I'm Your Boogie Man - 4 - 1

© 1976 EMI LONGITUDE MUSIC and HARRICK MUSIC, INC.
All Rights Reserved

aft-er-noon,___ or at mid-night, it's nev-er too soon {to want to / to want to

please you, to want to keep you; I want to do it all,___ all___ for___
take you, to want to hold you; I want to give my all,___ all___ to___

___ you. I want to be your, be your rub-ber ball.___ I want to
___ you. And I want you to com-plete-ly un-der-stand___ just

be the one__ you love most of all.
where I'm at__ and where I am. Oh, yeah.__

I'm your boo-gie man, I'm your boo-gie man,__ turn me on. I'm your

boo-gie man,_ I'm your boo-gie man,__ I'll do what you want.__ I'm your

3. I want to be with you, I want to be with you.
   Yeah, we'll be together, you and me.
   I want to see you; ah, get near you.
   I want to love you, ah, from sundown - sun up.
   Oh, yeah.

IT ONLY TAKES A MINUTE

Words and Music by
DENNIS LAMBERT and
BRIAN POTTER

Ah ha yeah, yeah

What's an hour of the day? We throw at least one away.
In the un-em-ploy-ment lines you can spend your life read-in' signs.

Walk the streets half a year,
Wait-in' for your in-ter-view, they can

© 1975 Universal - Duchess Music Corporation
All Rights Reserved

try-in' to find a new car-eer. Now if you, get a flu at-tack,
shoot the whole day for you. Now win-ters gon-na turn to spring,

for thir-ty days your on your back.
and you have-n't ac-com-plished a thing. So

Through the night I've seen you dance,
ba-by leave a lit-tle time 'cause you

ba-by give me half a chance. It on-ly takes a min-ute, girl,
nev-er know what's on my mind.

It Only Takes a Minute - 3 - 3

KNOCK ON WOOD

Words and Music by
EDDIE FLOYD and
STEVE CROPPER

Fast shuffle ♩ = 138

1. I___ don't wan-na

Knock on Wood - 5 - 1

© 1966 & 1973 IRVING MUSIC, INC. (BMI)
Copyright Renewed
All Rights Reserved

Verse:

lose you, this good__ thing that I got.__

2.3. *See additional lyrics*

'Cause if I do,__ I would sure-ly,

sure-ly lose a lot.__ 'Cause your love__ is bet-

ter than an-y love I__ know.__ It's like thun-

A
D
A
der, light - ning. The way you love me is fright -
D
N.C.
'ning. You bet - ter knock, knock, knock on wood,
3
3
3
3
Chorus:
A
C
D
E
G5
3
ba - by. Ooh,
E5
D5
5
C5
3
A
C
D
ba - by.

1.
E
G5
E5
D5
C5
A5
Ooh,
whoa.
2.3.
To Coda
A
D
2. I'm not su - per -
whoa.
Babe, you bet - ter knock, knock, knock on wood.
Babe, you bet - ter knock, knock, knock on wood.
Babe, you bet - ter
N.C.
Bm
C
knock.

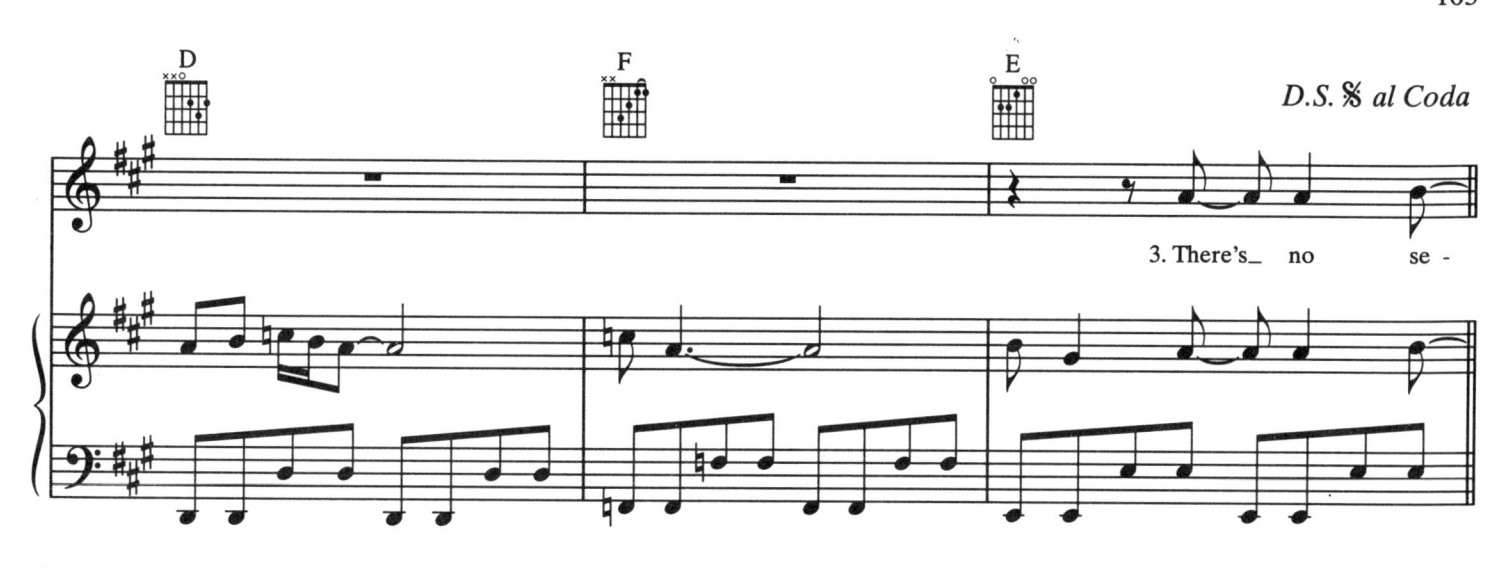

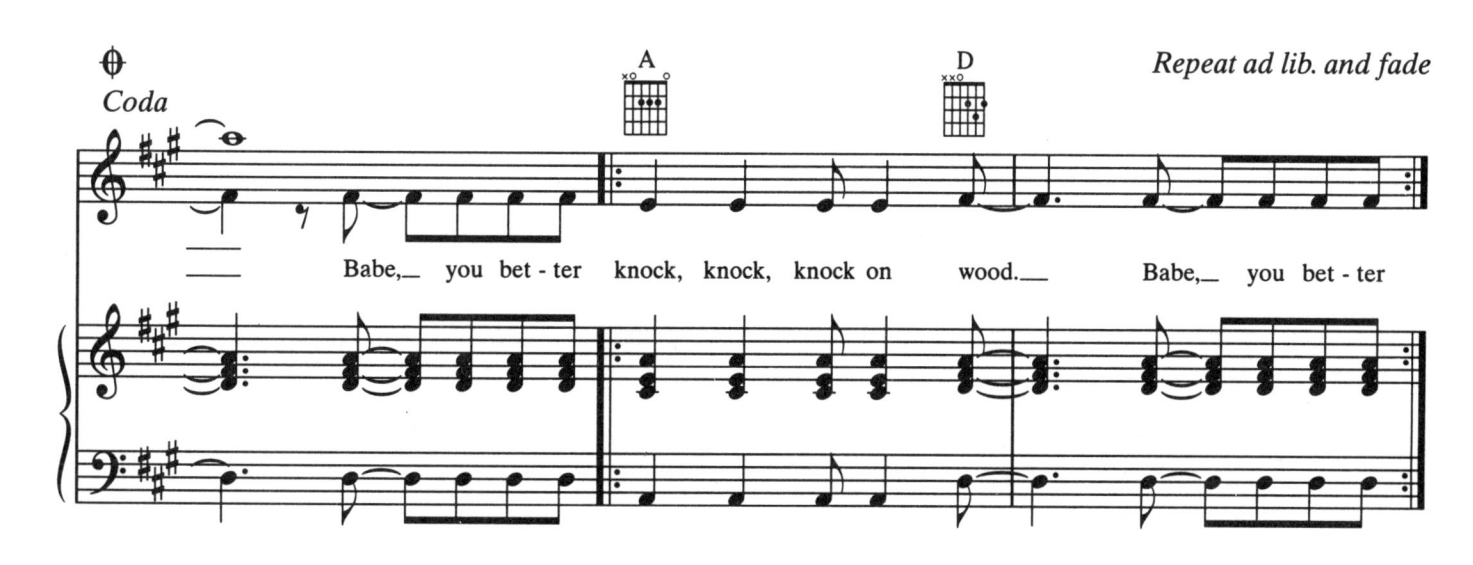

Verse 2:
I'm not superstitious about you
But I can't take no chance.
You got me spinnin', baby.
You know that I'm in a trance.
'Cause your love is better
Than any love I know.
It's like thunder, lightning.
The way you love me is frightening.
You better knock, knock, knock on wood.
(To Chorus:)

Verse 3:
There's no secret about it,
'Cause with his loving touch
He sees to it,
And I get enough.
Feel his touch all over.
You know it means so much.
It's like thunder, fast as lightning.
The way you love me is frightening.
You better knock, knock, knock on wood.
(To Chorus:)

JUNGLE BOOGIE

Words and Music by
RONALD BELL, CLAYDES SMITH,
ROBERT MICKENS, DONALD BOYCE,
RICHARD WESTERFIELD, DENNIS THOMAS,
ROBERT BELL and GEORGE BROWN

Moderate Rock

Get down, get down, get down, get down,
get down, get down, get down, get down.

Jungle Boogie - 2 - 1

© 1973 WARNER-TAMERLANE PUBLISHING CORP. and SECOND DECADE MUSIC CO.
All Rights on behalf of SECOND DECADE MUSIC CO. Administered by WARNER-TAMERLANE PUBLISHING CORP.
All Rights Reserved

105

Jun - gle boo - gie, jun - gle boo - gie (get it up)

D.S. to fade
2nd time

jun - gle boo - gie, jun - gle boo - gie. (growl)

IT'S RAINING MEN

Words and Music by
PAUL SHAFFER
and PAUL JABARA

Fast ♩ = 138

(Spoken:) Hi, we're your weather girls. And have we got news for you. You'd better listen. Get ready, all you lonely girls, and leave those umbrellas at home.

It's Raining Men - 8 - 1

© 1983 POSTVALDA MUSIC, MARTIN BANDIER MUSIC,
JONATHAN THREE MUSIC and CHARLES KOPPELMAN MUSIC
All Rights for POSTVALDA MUSIC Administered by W.B.M. MUSIC CORP.
All Rights Reserved

Verse 1:

1. The humidity's rising, the barometer's getting low. According to all sources, the street's the place to go. 'Cause tonight for the first time,

just a-bout half past ten, for the first time in his-tory, it's gon-na start rain-ing men. It's rain-ing men.

Chorus:
Hal-le-lu-jah! It's rain-ing men. A-men! I'm gon-na go out, I'm gon-na let my-self get

ab-so-lute-ly soak-ing wet. It's rain-ing men.

Hal-le-lu-jah! It's rain-ing men, ev-'ry spec-i-men: tall, blond, dark and lean,

rough and tough and strong and mean.

It's Raining Men - 8 - 5

Lyrics:

...and ev'ry woman could find the perfect guy.

Ooh, it's raining men, yeah!

Verse 2:
2. The humidity's rising, the ba-

rom-e-ter's get-ting low.

Ac-cord-ing to all sourc-es,

Csus

the street's the place to go.

C Fm

'Cause to-night for the first time,

just a-bout half past ten, for the first time in his-to-ry, it's gon-na start rain-ing men.

Chorus:
It's rain-ing men. Hal-le-lu-jah! It's rain-ing men. A-men! It's rain-ing men.

Repeat ad lib. and fade

KEEP IT COMIN' LOVE

Words and Music by
HARRY CASEY and RICHARD FINCH

Keep it com - in', love, keep it com - in', love. Don't stop it now, don't stop it, no. Don't stop it now, don't stop it. Keep it

Keep It Comin' Love - 4 - 1

© 1976 LONGITUDE MUSIC and HARRICK MUSIC, INC.
All Rights Reserved

comin', love, keep it comin', love. Don't stop it now, don't stop it, no. Don't stop it now, don't stop it.

Don't let your well run dry,
Don't build me up just to let me drop,
Don't tell me there ain't no more,
don't stop it now. Don't Don't

A♭maj7
Don't give me no rea - sons why,
turn me on just to turn me off,
turn me down and just close your door,
don't
B♭6
1.2.
3.
stop it now.
Keep it
Ooh, keep it
A♭maj7
com - in', love.
B♭6
Oh, yeah.

(Instrumental Solo)

1.2. 3. D.S. 𝄋 al Coda ⌖

Keep it

⌖ *Coda*   *Repeat and fade*

stop it now, don't stop it. Keep it com - in', love, keep it com - in', love. Keep it com - in', love, keep it com - in', love. Keep it

LADIES NIGHT

Words and Music by
GEORGE BROWN, ROBERT BELL,
RONALD BELL, JAMES TAYLOR,
EARL TOON, DENNIS THOMAS,
CLAYDES SMITH and MEEKAAEEL MUHAMMED

Moderate Disco beat

Oh yes, it's la-dies night and the feel-ing's right, oh yes, it's la-dies night, oh what a night. Oh yes, it's la-dies night and the feel-ing's right, oh yes, it's la-dies night, oh what a night.

Girl, y'all got one, a night that's spe-cial ev-'ry-where. From

Ladies Night - 4 - 1

© 1979 WARNER-TAMERLANE PUBLISHING CORP., SECOND DECADE MUSIC CO. and WB MUSIC CORP.
All Rights on behalf of SECOND DECADE MUSIC CO. Administered by WARNER-TAMERLANE PUBLISHING CORP.
All Rights Reserved

New York to Hollywood, it's ladies night and girl the feeling's good. Oh yes, it's ladies night and the feeling's right, oh yes, it's ladies night, oh what a night. Oh yes, it's ladies night and the feeling's right, oh yes, it's ladies night, oh what a night.

Romantic lady, single baby, mm, sophisticated ma-

Ladies Night - 4 - 2

ma. Come on, you disco lady, yeah, stay with me tonight, mama. If you hear any noise, it ain't the boys, it's ladies night, uh huh. Gonna step out ladies night, steppin' out ladies night. Gonna step out ladies night, steppin' out ladies night. Oh yes, it's

D. S. al Coda

Coda
C#m6
Am7
Bm7
Em7
Am7
On dis - co lights your name will be seen, you can ful - fill all
Bm7
Em7
Am7
Bm7
Em7
Am7
your dreams. Par - ty here, par - ty there, ev - 'ry - where, this is your night, ba - by, you've
Bm7
Em7
Repeat and fade
Cm7
Dm7
Gm7
got to be there. This is your night to - night, ev - 'ry - thing's gon - na be all right.
Cm7
Dm7
Gm7
This is your night to - night, ev - 'ry - thing's gon - na be all right.

MacARTHUR PARK

Moderately

Words and Music by
JIMMY WEBB

Spring was nev-er wait-ing for us,
I re-call the yel-low cot-ton

girl, it ran one step a-head as we fol-lowed in the
dress foam-ing like a wave on the ground a-round your

MacArthur Park - 10 - 1

© 1968 Canopy Music, Inc.
© Renewed and Assigned to Universal - PolyGram International Publishing, Inc.
All Rights Reserved

dance.
knees.
Be-
tween the part-ed pag-es__ and were pressed in love's__ hot fe-vered i-
birds like ten-der ba-bies__ in your hands and the old man play-ing cheq-
ron__ like a strip-ed pair__ of pants.
uers__ by the trees.

Mac-Ar-thur's Park is melt-ing in the dark,—

all the sweet green ic-ing flow-ing down. Some-one left the cake out in the rain; I don't think that I can take it 'cause it took so long to bake it and I'll nev-er have that rec-i-pe a-gain, oh, no.

There will be an-oth-er song for me, for I will sing it,

there will be an-oth-er dream for me, some-one will

bring___ it.___ I will drink the wine while it is warm___ and nev-er let you catch me look-ing at the sun,___ and af-ter all the loves___ of my life, af-ter all the loves___ of my life___ you'll still be the one. I will take my life ___ in-to my hands ___ and I will use ___ it, ___

I will win the wor-ship ___ in their eyes ___ and I ___ will lose ___ it: ___

I will have the things that I de-sire ___ and my pas-sion flow like

riv-ers to the sky, ___ and af-ter all the loves ___ of my

life, oh, af-ter all the loves of my life I'll be think-ing of you and won-der-ing why.

Double tempo
Gm
Am/G
Gm7
C/D
3 fr.
Am7
Dm7
G/D
5 fr.
7 fr.
8 fr.
E♭maj9
B♭maj7
F

Mac - Arthur's Park is melt-ing in the dark, all the sweet green ic-ing

Cm7 3 fr.
Cm7/F
F7-9 7 fr.
B♭
B♭maj7
C6
flow - ing down.
Some-one left the cake out in the rain;
I don't
Dm
F/C
Bm7-5
think that I can take it 'cause it took so long to bake it and I'll nev-er have that rec-i-pe a-
B♭m
F
A♭ 4 fr.
gain, oh, no.
Oh, no,
Fm
G♭
B♭sus4
B♭
B♭sus4
Fsus4
B♭
No, no, no, oh, no.
cresc.
rit.
ff

LADY LOVE

Words and Music by
YVONNE GRAY and
SHERMAN MARSHALL

Bright bossa feeling

La - dy___ Love,___
La - dy___ Love,___

your love is sooth - in' like the sum - mer's breeze.___
your love is cool - in' like the wint - er's snow.___

Lady Love - 7 - 1

© 1977 WARNER-TAMERLANE PUBLISHING CORP.
All Rights Reserved

My Lady Love,
My Lady Love,
your love is ten - der as a ba - by's touch,
your love is coz - y as a fire's glow,
And you give me all of the things that I
And I keep on need - ing you, girl, a lit - tle
need so much;
more and more;
You're my world, La - dy Love,
And I thank you, My La - dy Love.

Lady Love - 7 - 2

love.

(love) You know it's not eas-y to keep love go-in' smooth; Peo-ple are peo-ple and they

Lady Love - 7 - 3

Am
Am/G
F
all — have — their moods. —
But it's so
Em7
F
Em7
Dm7/G
nice to have some - one like you,
Who wants a
smooth and an eas - y thing —
and all the good times that it brings. My
and all the good times and the joy that it brings. My

Lady Love, you've been with
Lady Love, you've been with
me through all of my ups and downs.
me through all of my ups and downs
and my crazy turn a-rounds. My
you're my Lady Love,
Lady Love,
I once was lost but now with you I'm found;

F Am7/E To Coda Dm7 Dm7/G Am
You got the love I need and I want to stay a - round,
Am/G F F/E Dm7 Dm7/G C
Nev - er set you down, My La - dy Love.
C7
D.S. al Coda
Now let me tell you that
Coda Dm7 Dm7/G C
need my La - dy Love
feel to me
(Vocal ad libs)

Cmaj7
C7
F
Am7/E
Dm7
Dm7/G
(La - dy Love,)
I'm glad I found my
C
Cmaj7
La - dy Love
(La - dy Love)
C7
1.
F
Am7/E
Dm7
Dm7/G
3
I said like a warm summer breeze
I said I
that's how you
2.
F
Am7/E
Dm7
Dm7/G
C
love your ten - der touch, my La - dy Love.
rall

WHEN WILL I SEE YOU AGAIN

Words and Music by
KENNETH GAMBLE and LEON HUFF

*Vocal line at actual pitch

When Will I See You Again - 5 - 1

© 1974, 1982 WARNER-TAMERLANE PUBLISHING CORP.
All Rights Reserved

D7/4 E7/4
D7 E7
G A
precious moments...
When will I see
D/F# E/G#
Em F#m
Em/D F#m/E
you again?
C D
G/B A/C#
D7/4 E7/4
When will we share precious moments?
D7 E7
Bm C#m
Will I have to wait for -

Em
F♯m
ev - er?
Am7
Bm7
Will I have to suf - fer and
D7/4
E7/4
cry the whole night through?
D7
E7
N.C.
G
A
D/F♯
E/G♯
Em
F♯m
Em/D
F♯m/E
When will I see you a - gain?
C
D
G/B
A/C♯
D7/4
E7/4
D7
E7
When will our hearts be to-geth - er? Are we in
3

142

Bm / C#m *Em7 / F#m7*

love _____ or just friends? _____

Am7 / Bm7

Is this my be - gin - ning _____

D⁷₄ / E⁷₄ N.C.

or is this ___ the end? _____ When will I see you a-

G / A *C / D* *D / E* *G / A* To Coda

gain? (When will I see you a - gain?)

When Will I See You Again - 5 - 4

C D G D
D E A E
(harmony in small notes)
(When will I see you a - gain?)
Em Em7 C
F♯m F♯m7 D
Ha
G/D Am7 D7
A/E Bm7 E7
D.S. al Coda
Hoo pre - cious mo - ments . . .
Are we in
Coda
C D G
D E A
Repeat and fade
When will I see you a - gain?

LE FREAK

Words and Music by
NILE RODGERS and BERNARD EDWARDS

Medium Disco beat

Freak out! Le Freak, c'est chic. Freak out!

Freak

Have you heard a-
All that pres-sure

bout the new dance craze? Lis-ten to us. I'm sure you'll be a-mazed.
got you down; has your head spin-ning all a-round.

Am7
5fr.
D
5fr.
C6
3fr.
Am7
5fr.
Big fun to be had by ev - 'ry - one. It's up to you. It
Feel the rhy-thm. Chant the rhyme. Come on a - long and
D
5fr.
C6
3fr.
Am7
5fr.
sure - ly can be done. Young and old are
have a real good time. Like the days of
D
5fr.
C6
3fr.
Am7
5fr.
do - in' it, I'm told. Just one try and
stomp - in' at the Sa - voy, now we Freak.
D
5fr.
C6
3fr.
Am7
5fr.
you, too, will be sold. It's called "Le Freak." They're
Oh, what a joy. Just come on down

D C6 Am7 D C6
5fr. 3fr. 5fr. 5fr. 3fr.
do-in' it night and day.— Al-low us, we'll show you the way.—
to the Fif-ty-four.— Find a spot out on the floor.—
Freak
Am7 D C Am7
out! Le Freak, c'est chic. Freak out!
1. D C 2. D C
Repeat and fade
Am7
Freak out! Le
Repeat and fade
D C Am7 D C
Freak, c'est chic. Freak out! Freak

RING MY BELL

Words and Music by
FREDERICK KNIGHT

Moderately

I'm glad you're home. Now, did you really miss me? I guess
is young and full of possibilities. Well, come on

148

you did____ by that look in your eye.
and let____ your-self____ be free.

Well, lay back____ and re-lax____ while I
My love____ for you,____ so

put a-way the dish-es. Then you____ and me____
long I've been sav-ing. To-night____ was made____

Ring My Bell - 3 - 2

can rock-a - bye.
for me and you.
You can ring my bell, ring my bell.
You can ring my bell, ring my bell.
The night
You can ring my

ROCK THE BOAT

Words and Music by
WALLY HOLMES

Moderately, with a strong beat

So I'd like to know where you got the no-tion,— said I'd like to know where you got the

Rock the Boat - 5 - 1

© 1973, 1974 WARNER-TAMERLANE PUBLISHING CORP. and JIMI LANE MUSIC
All Rights Reserved

no - tion __ to rock the boat, don't rock _ the boat, ba - by, rock the boat, don't tip _ the boat o - ver, rock the boat, don't rock _ the boat, ba - by, rock the boat. _____

Ev - er since _ our voy - age of love be - gan, __ your
up to now _ we've sailed _ through ev - 'ry storm __ and I've

touch has thrilled me like the rush of the wind. And your
al - ways had your ten - der lips to keep me warm. Oh, I

arms have held me safe from a roll - ing sea; there's
need to have the strength that flows from you; don't

al - ways been a qui - et place to har - bor you and me.
let me drift a - way, my dear, when love can see me through.

Our love is like a ship on the o -

cean.___ we've been sail-ing with a car-go full of love and de-vo-tion. So I'd like to know___ where you got the no-tion,___ said I'd like to know___ where you got the no-tion___ to rock the boat, don't rock the boat, ba-by, rock the boat, don't tip the boat o-ver,

rock the boat, don't rock the boat, ba-by, rock the boat.

rock the boat, don't tip the boat o-ver.

Repeat and fade

Rock the boat, rock the boat.

Repeat and fade

(Shake, Shake, Shake)
SHAKE YOUR BOOTY

Moderate Disco Beat

Words and Music by
HARRY WAYNE CASEY
and RICHARD FINCH

Aw,
1. Ev-'ry-bo-dy get on the floor, let's dance.
2. You can, you can do it ver-y well.

Don't fight the feel-in', give your-self a chance.
You're the best in the world, I can tell.

(Shake, Shake, Shake) Shake Your Booty - 5 - 1

© 1976 EMI LONGITUDE MUSIC and HARRICK MUSIC, INC.
All Rights Reserved

Ab
4th fret
Bb
Shake, shake, shake,
shake, shake, shake,
shake your
Cm
Ab
4th fret
boo - ty
Shake your boo - ty.
Shake, shake, shake,
Bb
Cm
to Coda
Shake, shake, shake,
shake your boo - ty.
Shake your boo - ty.
Aw,
Cm
F7
1.
Shake, shake
shake, shake,

157

shake, shake, shake your boo-ty. — You can do it, do it.

Shake, shake, shake, shake, shake your boo-ty. — Come on ma-ma. Shake, shake, shake, shake, shake your boo-ty. — Woo, woo, woo,

woo, woo, woo, woo, woo, woo, woo, Shake, shake, shake, shake, shake your boo-ty.— Aw, drop down, sis-ter.

Shake, shake, come on. Shake, shake, come on your boo-ty.— Aw, your boo-ty.—

Repeat and fade

SHAKE YOUR GROOVE THING

Words and Music by
DINO FEKARIS and FREDDIE PERREN

Bright, with a steady beat
no chord

Opt. 8va bassa throughout

Shake__ it! Shake it!

Shake Your Groove Thing - 7 - 1

© 1978, 1979 Universal - PolyGram International Publishing, Inc. and Perren-Vibes Music Inc.
All Rights Reserved

A
C/A
Bm7/A
Shake your groove thing, shake your groove thing, yeah, yeah!
Bm7/E
Show 'em how you do it now.
A
C/A
Bm7/A
Shake your groove thing, shake your groove thing, yeah, yeah!
no chord
Show 'em how you do it now, show 'em how you do it now.

Shake Your Groove Thing

[A] Let's show the world we can dance, **[C/A]** **[Bm7/A]** bad enough ta
We've got the rhythm tonight, all the rest know

[Bm7/E] strut our stuff. **[A]** The music gives us a chance, **[C/A]**
we're the best. Our shadows flash in the light,

[Bm7/A] we do more out on the floor. **[F#m]** Groovin' loose
twistin' turnin', we keep burnin'. Shake it high

[G] or heart to heart, **[Bm7/E]** we put in motion ev'ry single part.
or shake it low, we take our bodies where they want to go.

Funk-y sounds wall to wall, we're bump-in' boot-ies, hav-
Feel the beat, nev-er stop, oh, hold me tight, spin

in' us a ball, y'all.
me like a top!

Shake your groove thing, shake your groove thing, yeah, yeah! Show 'em how you do it now.

Shake your groove thing, shake your groove thing, yeah, yeah!

To Coda ⊕

no chord

Show 'em how you do it now.

D.S. al Coda

CODA ⊕

no chord

'em how you do it now. There's noth-ing more that

D

I'd like to do than take the floor and dance with you. Keep danc-in', let's keep danc-in'.

Shake it'! Shake it! Groov-in' loose

Shake Your Groove Thing - 7 - 6

or heart to heart, we put in mo-tion ev-'ry sin-gle part. Funk-y sounds wall to wall, we're bump-in' boot-ies hav-in' us a ball, y'all. Shake your groove thing, shake your groove thing, yeah, yeah! Show 'em how you do it now.

Repeat and Fade

TURN THE BEAT AROUND

Words and Music by
PETER JR. JACKSON
and GERALD JACKSON

Fast ♩ = 132

© 1975 UNICHAPPELL MUSIC, INC.
All Rights Reserved

168

%S *Chorus:*

Turn the beat a-round. Love to hear per-cus-sion. Turn it up-side down.

Love to hear per-cus-sion. Love to hear it.

Verse:

1. Blow, horn, you sure sound pret-ty. Your vi-o-lins keep mov-ing to the nit-ty grit-
2. Flute play-er, play your flute 'cause I know you wan-na get your thing

Turn the Beat Around - 5 - 2

Bridge:

'Cause when the gui-tar play-er stars play-in' with the syn-co-pa-ted rhy-thm, with the scratch, scratch, scratch

(lyrics above bridge:)
ty. And when you hear the scratch of the gui-tar scratch-
off. But, you see, I've made my mind up 'bout

in', then you know that rhy-thm car-ries all the ac-
it. Got to be the rhythm, no doubt a-bout

1. tion. Oh, yeah.
2. it. Oh.

Turn the Beat Around - 5 - 3

makes me wan-na move my bod-y, yeah, yeah, yeah.

And when the drum-mer starts beat-in' that beat, beat-in' out that beat with the syn-co-pa-ted rhy-thm with a

rat-tat-tat-ta-tat-tat on the drums. Hey!

D.S. 𝄋 al Coda

⊕ Coda

Love to hear it. Love to hear it. Love to hear it.

(Percussion Solo)

F#m N.C. Am7/D *Play 5 times*

Chorus:

Gm F Eb F

Turn the beat__ a-round.__ Love to hear__ per-cus-

Gm F Eb

sion. Turn it up-side down.__

F Gm *Repeat ad lib. and fade*

Love to hear__ per-cus-sion.

WE ARE FAMILY

Words and Music by
NILE RODGERS and BERNARD EDWARDS

Moderately

[A7] [G(addA)] [D] [F/G]

We are fam - i - ly.   I got all my sis-ters with me.

[A7] [G(addA)] [D] [F/G]

We are fam - i - ly.   Get up, ev-'ry-bod-y, and sing.

[A] [Em7] [D9] [A] [Em7]

Ev - 'ry - one can see we're to - geth - er   as we walk

© 1979 BERNARD'S OTHER MUSIC and TOMMY JYMI, INC.
All Rights Administered by WARNER-TAMERLANE PUBLISHING CORP.
All Rights Reserved

D9
4fr.
A
Em7
D9
4fr.
A
Em7
on by._ And we flock just like birds_ of a feath - er. I won't tell
D9
4fr.
A
Em7
D9
4fr.
A
Em7
no lie._ All of the peo - ple a - round us, they say,_ "Can they be_
D9
4fr.
A
Em7
D9
4fr.
A
Em7
_ that close?" Just let me state for the rec - ord: We're giv - ing love in a fam -
D9
4fr.
A7
G(addA)
D
F/G
'ly dose. We are fam - i - ly. I got all my sis - ters with me.

We are fam-i-ly. Get up, ev-'ry-bod-y, and sing. Liv-ing life is fun, and we've just be-gun to get our share of this world's de-lights. High hopes we have for the fu-ture. And our goal's in sight. No, we don't get de-pressed. Here's what we call *our* golden rule: Have faith in you and the things you do. You won't go wrong. This is our fam-'ly jewel.

Repeat and fade

We are fam-i-ly. I got all my sis-ters with me.

We are fam-i-ly. Get up, ev-'ry-bod-y, and sing.

TSOP (THE SOUND OF PHILADELPHIA)

Moderate, straight ahead 4

Words and Music by
KENNETH GAMBLE
and LEON HUFF

© 1973 WARNER-TAMERLANE PUBLISHING CORP. and HIP TRIP MUSIC CO.
All Rights Administered by WARNER-TAMERLANE PUBLISHING CORP.
All Rights Reserved

TSOP - 4 - 1

Am C Am C Am C Am C
Cm E♭ Cm E♭ Cm E♭ Cm E♭
Am C Am C Am C Am C
Cm E♭ Cm E♭ Cm E♭ Cm E♭
Am C Am C Am C
Cm E♭ Cm E♭ Cm E♭
Am C D E
Cm E♭ F G
gliss

C
Eb
To Coda
D
F
E
G
A
C
F♮m
Am
Dmaj7/E
Fmaj7/G
A
C
F♮m
Am
Dmaj7/E
Fmaj7/G
D.S. al Coda
C
Eb
Coda
D
F
E
G
Am
Cm
Play 2 times

Am
Cm
Play 2 times
Am
Cm
D
F
Play 4 times
opt.
Am
Cm
D
F
Play 2 times
Am
Cm
D
F
Play 2 times
Doot doot doot n doo doo
Doo doot
Am
Cm
D
F
Am
Cm
D
F
Doot doot doot-n - doo doo
doo - doo - doo
etc.
What's go - in'
Am
Cm
D
F
Am
Cm
D
F
Repeat and fade
on?
It's time to get down.
What's go - in'

I LOVE MUSIC

Words and Music by
KENNETH GAMBLE
and LEON HUFF

Moderate *

*4 bar percussion intro. omitted.

© 1975 WARNER-TAMERLANE PUBLISHING CORP.
All Rights Reserved

I love mu - sic, _____ an - y kind of mu - sic,

I love mu - sic, _____ just as long_

_____ as it's groov - y. Makes me laugh makes me smile all the

while when - ev - er I'm with you, _____ girl. _____ I will

dance, make ro-mance, I'm en-chant-ed by the things that you do.

Oh_____ wo___ wo___ wo___ wo_____

I love mu-sic,_____ sweet,___ sweet mu-sic,

All that's swing-ing, ____ all the joy ____ that it's bring-ing. ____ I'm so hap-py to be in com-plete har-mo-ny, I love you, girl. As I hold you so close in my arms I'm so glad that you're mine all ____ mine ____

Nothing can be better than a sweet love song (So sweet, so sweet, so mellow, mellow) When you got the girl that you love in your arms.

Honey, I love you, I love you, yeah!

Music is the healing force of the world

Fm7 Gm7 Fm7 Gm7 Fm7 Gm7
It's un - der - stood by ev - 'ry man, wom-an, boy and girl.
Fm7 Gm7 Fm7 Gm7 Fm7 Gm7
And that's why I say: I love mu - sic,
Fm7 Gm7 Fm7 Gm7 Fm7 Gm7
an - y kind of mu - sic.
Fm7 Gm7 Fm7 Gm7 Fm7 Gm7
I love mu - sic, just as long as it's groov - y.

Mu-sic makes the an - kles feel so fine,

(Lights down low just near you, ba-by, you know) Spec-'ly when we got a full

glass of wine. I know, glass of wine, that's all.

Repeat and fade

Coda

(Pianist: omit vocal melody)
I love, I love, I love, I love, I love mu - sic...

WB Music Presents
The Complete Collection Series

BROADWAY MUSIC
(F3468SMX)
Contains 73 memorable songs, *including*: Give My Regards to Broadway (*George M!*) • Cabaret (*Cabaret*) • Do Nothin' Till You Hear From Me (*Sophisticated Ladies*) • Ease on Down the Road (*The Wiz*) • Forty-Second Street (*42nd Street*) • The Lady Is a Tramp (*Pal Joey*) • Tomorrow (*Annie*) and many more.

CHRISTMAS MUSIC
(F3350SMC)
Contains 125 favorite popular and traditional Christmas songs in one beautiful collection. *Titles include*: Christmas Eve in My Home Town • Christmas Time Is Here (from "A Charlie Brown Christmas") • Gesu Bambino (The Infant Jesus) • God Rest Ye Merry, Gentlemen • The Hawaiian Christmas Song • Winter Wonderland.

COUNTRY MUSIC
(F3284SMB)
This collection contains 91 of the most requested country songs ever recorded. *Titles include*: The Dance • Don't Take the Girl • Forever's As Far As I'll Go • I Will Always Love You • If Tomorrow Never Comes • Love, Me • The Vows Go Unbroken (Always True to You) • The Yellow Rose of Texas • Your Cheatin' Heart.

HAWAIIAN MUSIC
(MF9923)
The most comprehensive resource to date! Sixty-nine titles, *including*: Across the Sea • Aloha Land • Aloha Means I Love You • Hawaiian Butterfly • Hawaiian War Chant (Ta-Hu-Wa-Hu-Wa) • Hilo E • Kalamaula • Lei Ohu • Love Song of Kalua • Maunaloa • My Little Grass Shack in Kealakekua Hawaii • On the Beach at Waikiki and more.

JAZZ MUSIC
(F3336SMB)
Eighty-nine classic jazz greats spanning the years of Duke Ellington to Stevie Wonder. *Titles include*: Do Nothin' Till You Hear From Me • Embraceable You • Laura • Misty • Moonglow • On Green Dolphin Street • Prelude to a Kiss • Satin Doll • Sir Duke • Toot Toot Tootsie (Goodbye) • Take Five • You Are the Sunshine of My Life.

MOVIE MUSIC
(F3325SMX)
Ninety-two of the most famous songs ever written for motion pictures. *Includes*: End of the Road • The Greatest Love of All • Heart of a Hero • (Everything I Do) I Do It for You • I Will Always Love You • I'm Every Woman • I'd Do Anything • Over the Rainbow • Theme from *Ice Castles* (Through the Eyes of Love) • Up Where We Belong.

NEW AGE MUSIC
(F3462P9X)
A complete collection of 64 titles from our most popular writers, such as Michael Scott, Chris Lobdell, Joseph Scianni, Derek Kieran and Edwin McLean. *Titles include*: Across the Dunes • Conversations on the Beach • Dance of the Mountain Bluebells • Miss Emily's Attic • Music Box • On North Riverside • Quiet Moments • Where Butterflies Hide.

LA NUEVA COLECCION DE MUSICA LATINA
(MF9814)
Seventy-one great Latin hits from such artists as Luis Miguel, Tito Puente, Ray Barretto, Eddie Palmieri, Santana and more! *Titles include*: Guantanamera • La Bamba • La Cucaracha • Laura • Cielito Lindo (Beautiful Heaven) • Conga • Tequila • Oye Como Vá • Mi Casa • Mexican Hat Dance • Macarena • No Me Vuelvo a Enamorar.

ROCK MUSIC
(MF9644A)
Titles include: After Midnight • Basket Case • Change the World • Come to My Window • A Horse with No Name • Hotel California • Jack & Diane • Light My Fire • Longview • More Than Words • Stairway to Heaven • Streets of Philadelphia • Stupid Girl • Tears in Heaven • Til I Hear It From You • The World I Know and many more!

ROCK 'N' ROLL
(F3429SMB)
Nearly 100 titles made famous by classic artists like Little Richard, Elvis, Creedence Clearwater Revival, The Everly Brothers, The Doors and The Beatles. *Includes*: Bad Moon Rising • Bye, Bye Love • Good Golly Miss Molly • The House of the Rising Sun • Let the Good Times Roll • Oh, Pretty Woman.

WEDDING MUSIC
(F3222SMD)
A comprehensive collection ideal for the pianist who plays for wedding services or receptions. Includes music which rarely appears in wedding publications, such as Jewish wedding music that is difficult to find but is often requested. *Titles Include*: Ave Maria (Schubert) • Hava Nagila • Here and Now • We've Only Just Begun.

WARNER BROS. PUBLICATIONS
BEST SELLING FOLIOS

THE GREATEST POP HITS OF 1999 SO FAR
(MF9913)

A collection of the greatest pop songs from the first half of 1999. *Titles (and artists) include:* All I Have to Give (Backstreet Boys) • Angel of Mine (Monica) • ...Baby One More Time (Britney Spears) • Believe (Cher) • Crush (Jennifer Paige) • Duel of the Fates (from *Star Wars: Episode I The Phantom Menace*) (John Williams) and more.

GREATEST COUNTRY HITS OF 1999 SO FAR
(MF9914)

A collection of the best country music from the first half of 1999. Features artists such as Garth Brooks, Faith Hill, George Strait, Clint Black, Alan Jackson, Steve Wariner, Tim McGraw, Shania Twain, Billy Ray Cyrus, Vince Gill, and more. *Titles include:* Burnin' the Roadhouse Down • Fly (The Angel Song) • From This Moment On • Hole in the Floor of Heaven • It's Your Song • Love Ain't Like That.

SMASH POP HITS 1998-1999
(MF9903)

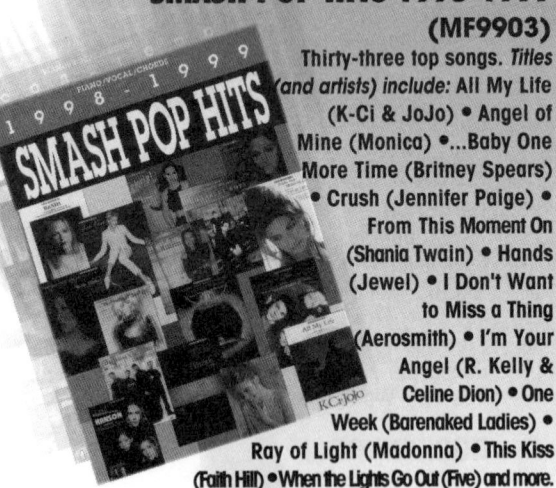

Thirty-three top songs. *Titles (and artists) include:* All My Life (K-Ci & JoJo) • Angel of Mine (Monica) • ...Baby One More Time (Britney Spears) • Crush (Jennifer Paige) • From This Moment On (Shania Twain) • Hands (Jewel) • I Don't Want to Miss a Thing (Aerosmith) • I'm Your Angel (R. Kelly & Celine Dion) • One Week (Barenaked Ladies) • Ray of Light (Madonna) • This Kiss (Faith Hill) • When the Lights Go Out (Five) and more.

SMASH COUNTRY HITS 1998-1999
(MF9904)

Forty top songs *Titles (and artists) include:* Holes in the Floor of Heaven (Steve Wariner) • From This Moment On (Shania Twain) • This Kiss (Faith Hill) • 26¢ (The Wilkinsons) • There's Your Trouble (Dixie Chicks) • Loosen Up My Strings (Clint Black) • If You Ever Have Forever in Mind (Vince Gill) • It's Your Song (Garth Brooks) • You're Easy on the Eyes (Terri Clark) • It Must Be Love (Ty Herndon) and many more!

THE GREATEST LOVE SONGS OF THE 90s
(MF9902)

Fifty-seven hit love songs from the world's top artists. *Titles (and artists) include:* I'm Your Angel (R. Kelly & Celine Dion) • Me and You (Kenny Chesney) • More Than Words (Extreme) • You Were Meant for Me (Jewel) • You're Still the One (Shania Twain) • This Kiss (Faith Hill) • Valentine (Jim Brickman) • All My Life (K-Ci and JoJo) • Because You Loved Me (Celine Dion) • How Do I Live (LeAnn Rimes) • Dreaming of You (Selena) and more.

SMASH POP HITS 1999-2000 Special Edition
(MF9929)

Titles (and artists) include: All Star (Smash Mouth) • As Long As You Love Me (Backstreet Boys) • Back at One (Brian McKnight) • (You Drive Me) Crazy (Britney Spears) • From This Moment On (Shania Twain) • Genie in a Bottle (Christina Aguilera) • I Will Remember You (Sarah McLachlan) • (God Must Have Spent) A Little More Time on You (*NSYNC) • No Scrubs (TLC) • She's All I Ever Had (Ricky Martin) and many more.

SMASH COUNTRY HITS 1999-2000 Special Edition
(MF9928)

Titles (and artists) include: Almost Home (Mary Chapin Carpenter) • Anyone Else (Collin Raye) • Big Deal (LeAnn Rimes) • Come on Over (Shania Twain) • Give My Heart to You (Billy Ray Cyrus) • Her (Aaron Tippin) • Holes in the Floor of Heaven (Steve Wariner) • It Don't Matter to the Sun (Garth Brooks as Chris Gaines) and many, many more.